CONTENTS

Introduction 2

Arguments against going to space
Space flight is bad for the body 6
Space flight is dangerous 8
Space pollution 12
Dangerous microbes 14
Dangerous asteroids 16

Arguments for going to space
Useful scientific discoveries 20
Understanding more about the Solar System 24
Forecasting the weather 25
Finding new natural resources 26
New life forms in space 28

Summing up 30
Glossary 31
Index 32

INTRODUCTION

The Earth belongs to a family of nine planets that make up the Solar System. The Solar System is part of a **galaxy** called the Milky Way. The Milky Way is about 950,000,000,000,000,000 kilometres wide. It is only one of millions of galaxies that make up the universe.

☆ The Milky Way

Over the years scientists have worked hard to discover more about space. They have made many discoveries using satellites and spacecraft. The distances involved make space exploration very complicated. The light reaching the Earth from the nearest star (after the Sun) would have set off nearly four years ago. To travel to this star and return would take a rocket thousands of years.

People have already learned a lot about the Solar System, but there is still a great deal to discover about space. But is exploring space worth all the risks, dangers and huge amounts of money that are spent?

Neil Armstrong was the first human being to walk on the Moon. It cost the USA $24,000,000,000 to send him up there in July 1969. He and his fellow astronauts collected rock samples, took photographs, and set up experiments to monitor the Moon's activity and environment. But was the trip worth it?

In 1969 only two countries were able to explore space – the USA and the Soviet Union. These days Argentina, Australia, Brazil, Britain, Canada, China, France, Germany, India, Israel, Japan, Sweden, and many other countries spend money on space exploration.

Now NASA (the National Aeronautics and Space Administration) is thinking about sending people to Mars. Nobody is quite sure yet what that will cost. But it is going to make the cost of landing on the Moon look cheap!

Do you honestly think that going into space is worth it?

SPACE FLIGHT IS BAD FOR THE BODY

The effects of **gravity** are much smaller in space than they are on the Earth. This means that people's muscles and bones get weaker because it takes less effort to lift and to move things. People's faces puff up, and their body clocks (which tell them when they need to sleep) get confused. In space bodies start to **dehydrate**. People will probably get backache. Their intestines move into a different place. They will feel as if they have a cold.

Unless astronauts are very lucky, they get space sickness (experts call it 'space adaptation syndrome'). That means loss of appetite, cold sweats, dizziness and sickness, all of which can start about an hour after the launch.

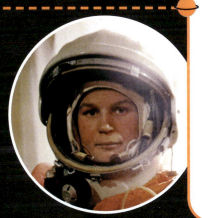

☆ Valentina Tereshkova, the first woman in space, suffered terrible space sickness.

These are the physical problems experienced. There are also emotional problems. For example, the astronaut Buzz Aldrin, who went to the Moon in 1969 with Neil Armstrong, had a nervous breakdown when he came back. Travelling in space changed him forever.

☆ Buzz Aldrin also suffered from his trip to space.

SPACE FLIGHT IS DANGEROUS

Travelling in space brings astronauts into contact with lots of radiation. Despite taking precautions, the crew of the US *Skylab* mission picked up nearly 18 units of radiation (rads) in just eighty-four days. Too much radiation can cause cancer. Some experts think 100 rads are too much. Others think that even 50 rads are too much. A long-haul space flight certainly puts people in the danger zone.

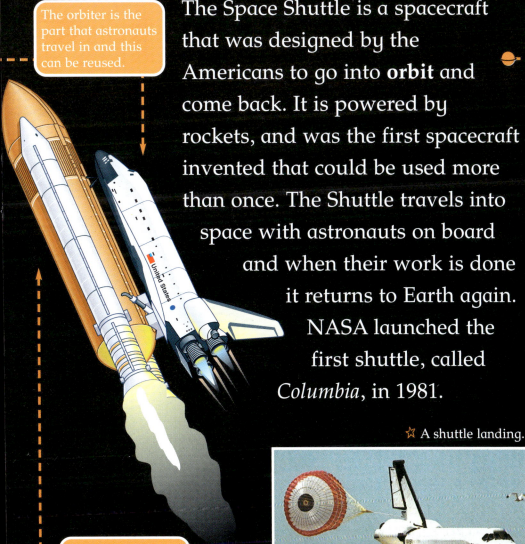

> The orbiter is the part that astronauts travel in and this can be reused.

The Space Shuttle is a spacecraft that was designed by the Americans to go into **orbit** and come back. It is powered by rockets, and was the first spacecraft invented that could be used more than once. The Shuttle travels into space with astronauts on board and when their work is done it returns to Earth again. NASA launched the first shuttle, called *Columbia*, in 1981.

☆ A shuttle landing.

> The booster rockets which carry the fuel last for only one space flight.

But is it always safe?

In 1985, NASA thought it would be a good idea to let an ordinary person take a space flight. Until then, the only people to go into space had been trained astronauts. NASA held a competition to find this 'amateur' astronaut, with a Shuttle ticket as the prize. A teacher won it. Her name was Christa McAuliffe.

On 28 January 1986, Christa joined the astronauts aboard the Space Shuttle *Challenger*. There were seven people on board altogether.

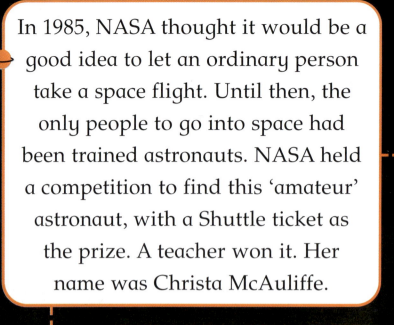

Two minutes after lift-off, it exploded. Christa and everybody else on board was killed. Flames had got into the main fuel tank and the Shuttle exploded like a bomb.

 Surely we should not put people into space if it means risking their lives?

11

SPACE POLLUTION

Countries have launched so many **satellites** that some people think it is like a junk-yard in space. In most cases, satellites burn up in the Earth's **atmosphere**. But a few old satellites break up, and parts of them make it all the way back to Earth every year.

Should we really put more of our rubbish into space? Sooner or later one of the pieces from a satellite is going to land on somebody.

DANGEROUS MICROBES

There may be bugs out there! Some scientists believe our worst plagues and diseases may have started when microbes or tiny germs carried by meteorites reached the Earth. Also there may be things on Earth that would harm space if they were taken there. Space scientists have to make sure that no Earth microbes pollute the Moon or Mars when spacecraft go there.

Astronauts have to be very careful when they collect samples.

But what would happen if human beings started to make regular round trips into space? If microbes can survive a trip through space – and there are clear signs that they can – then the Earth could face a strange disease from outer space. We may not have any defence at all against such a disease.

In the fourteenth century, about a third of the total population of Europe died when a plague called the Black Death hit Europe. That was about 75,000,000 people.

 A plague from outer space could be even worse than the Black Death.

DANGEROUS ASTEROIDS

Asteroids are lumps of rock orbiting the Sun. In the Solar System they are found mainly between Mars and Jupiter. **Astronomers** used to think they were the remains of an exploded planet. Some still do, but most now think that an asteroid is a planet starting to form.

Asteroid belt

Earth-killer asteroids are much bigger than the others

Asteroids can get quite big. Ceres, the largest that has been found, is nearly 1,000 kilometres in diameter. There are literally millions of asteroids that are as big as boulders.

We know that ninety-one of these asteroids regularly cross the Earth's orbit. We also know that there are at least 250 'Earth-killer' asteroids in space. An 'Earth-killer' asteroid is one that is big enough to destroy Earth and is close enough to hit Earth.

Some astronomers estimate there are more than 2,200 'Earth-killer' asteroids still waiting to be found.

Scientists already have several plans about what could be done about Earth-killer asteroids.

- A mirror could be built to orbit the Earth. This would be used to focus the rays of the Sun like a laser and destroy the asteroid completely.

- Powerful rocket motors could be put on the surface of the asteroid to change its course so that it missed the Earth.

- It has even been suggested that enormous 'sails' should be attached to the asteroid. These would catch the solar wind (the stream of particles given off by the Sun) and move the asteroid away from the Earth.

Since most asteroids are small, these plans could work. But the plans all have one thing in common: someone has to go into space to put them into action.

A meteorite is a tiny asteroid that finds its way to Earth. It makes a bright streak of light in the sky as it comes through the Earth's atmosphere. Even a small one can do a lot of damage if it hits the ground.

USEFUL SCIENTIFIC DISCOVERIES

There are also lots of good reasons to explore space.

Many scientific discoveries have been made because of experiments done on space missions. These discoveries include new medicines, ways to grow plants, and new equipment.

In space and away from other planets, there is less gravity than on Earth. This makes it easier to mix things together. On Earth when we add sand to water the sand sinks to the bottom and does not mix. In space it does not sink. Space is ideal for many experiments that involve mixing chemicals.

Growing crystals on Earth can be difficult because things are constantly bombarded by dust particles and gas molecules in the air. In space this is not a problem as there are very few particles or even molecules. Space is an almost perfect **vacuum**.

Medical equipment has been developed from experiments done on space missions. For example, a special light probe which was used as part of an experiment on the Space Shuttle, is now being used to help to cure cancer.

Light probe

An experiment done in space tested new ways of growing plants. The results could help us to produce more food for the people in the world.

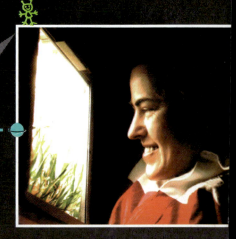

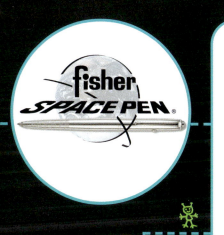

Do you have a ball-point pen that writes even when it is held upside down? If you do, it might be based on a pen that was developed on a mission to the Moon!

Going to the Moon meant that scientists had to invent new materials that were light, strong and could stand extremely hot and cold temperatures. These materials have also been used on aeroplanes.

UNDERSTANDING MORE ABOUT THE SOLAR SYSTEM

Exploring space helps us to learn more about the Solar System that we live in. For example, by putting a special telescope into space in 1985, NASA scientists were able to measure how much helium gas there is in the outer layers of the Sun.

Human beings have always been fascinated by space and the stars and planets, and it is important that we understand that our Earth is part of a much bigger Solar System. Whatever we do on Earth could affect the Solar System around us too.

FORECASTING THE WEATHER

Every day people eagerly listen to weather forecasts. Recently **meteorologists** have made great use of weather satellites. Two types of satellite are used:
- Orbiting satellites that regularly go around the Earth.
- Geo-stationary satellites that stay in one place 36,000 kilometres above the **equator**.

Weather satellites show weather patterns that cannot be predicted or seen from the Earth.

FINDING NEW NATURAL RESOURCES

There are over six billion people in the world today. By the year 2042, there could be nearly twice that number.

Because there are so many people on the planet, we are using up the Earth's natural resources very fast. Stocks of coal and oil are already running low. Copper, which we started using in 8000 BC, is very scarce.

If the population doubles (and triples not too long after that) just about everything will be running out. One answer to this problem would be to find the materials we need somewhere outside the planet.

Scientists are working hard to find out what asteroids are made of. We know they are mostly made of rock, but there is iron in them too and there may well be other valuable metals as well. So we could start mining asteroids.

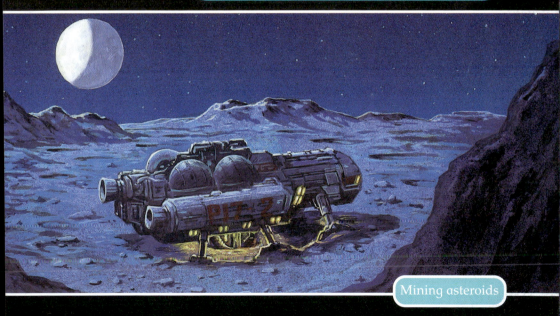

Mining asteroids

We will only make these discoveries if we continue to explore space.

NEW LIFE FORMS IN SPACE

We might find life out there.

In 1976, NASA put two landers down on Mars. They were designed to look for signs of life. They carried out three experiments. All three had positive results.

On 6 August 1996, another team of NASA scientists announced they had also discovered evidence of life on Mars. They had found a 4,500,000,000 year old meteorite that came from Mars. Inside it were the fossils of tiny life forms.

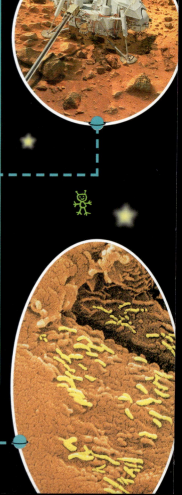

Since then, scientists have found evidence of rivers, streams and oceans on Mars. That means it certainly *could* have supported life at one time. Some people think it could also do so in the future.

Life on Mars?

SUMMING UP

So do you think we should stay at home or strike out even deeper into space?

- What good things do you think have come out of the explorations into space?
- Do you think we might one day be able to cure diseases using drugs made from alien plants grown on a distant planet?
- Do you think we have enough problems on Earth without looking for more in outer space?
- Perhaps you think we should compromise – explore the Moon and maybe Mars, set up something to deflect the 'Earth-killer asteroids', but go no further?

There are all sorts of options, but one thing is certain. You will have to help make those decisions when you grow up. So you might as well start thinking about them now!

GLOSSARY

astronomer	scientist who studies space
atmosphere	the air around the Earth
dehydrate	lose water
equator	an imaginary belt around the middle of the Earth
galaxy	a group of planets, stars, etc. held together by gravity
gravity	a force (on the Earth gravity pulls things to the ground)
meteorologist	a person who measures and forecasts the weather
orbit	the path of an object as it moves through space around another object
satellite	an object in space that moves around another object
vacuum	a perfectly empty space

Aldrin, Buzz 7
Armstrong, Neil 4
asteroids 16-19, 27
astronauts 6-7

Challenger Space Shuttle 10-11
choices for space exploration 30
cost of space exploration 4-5

destroying killer asteroids 18
diseases 14-15

Earth-killer asteroids 17-19
experiments in space 20-23

germs from space 14-15
gravity 6, 21

heat-resistant materials 23

life on Mars 28-29
light from stars 3

McAuliffe, Christa 10-11

Mars 28-29
medical advances 22
meteorites 19
Milky Way, the 2
Moon landing 4

NASA 5
natural resources 26-27

plant growth 22
pollution in space 12-13
population of Earth 26

radiation 8

satellites 12-13, 25
Solar System 2, 24
Space Shuttles 9-11
space sickness 5-6

telescopes 24

vacuum 21

weather forecasts 25